MY 30-DAY

Reset

JOURNAL

MY 30-DAY

Reset

JOURNAL

ACHIEVE YOUR FITNESS GOALS AND CREATE POSITIVE HABITS

SANDY JOY WESTON

Skyhorse Publishing

Skyhorse Publishing books may be purchased in bulk at special discounts for sales promotion, corporate gifts, fund-raising, or educational purposes. Special editions can also be created to specifications. For details, contact the Special Sales Department, Skyhorse Publishing, 307 West 36th Street, 11th Floor, New York, NY 10018 or info@skyhorsepublishing.com.

Skyhorse® and Skyhorse Publishing® are registered trademarks of Skyhorse Publishing, Inc.®, a Delaware corporation.

Visit our website at www.skyhorsepublishing.com.

10 9 8 7 6 5 4 3 2 1

Library of Congress Cataloging-in-Publication Data is available on file.

Cover design by Qualcom

Print ISBN: 978-1-5107-4682-4

Printed in China

Dedication

I am beyond thankful to my inner voice—my higher power—that I connect with every day
and is with me every step of the way to live a life of joy and speak my truth.

I also feel very blessed to have family and friends who support me, guide me, and push me forward,
even when they have no idea what I am talking about or what I am trying to do.
I send you all much love, joy, and fun.

Oh, I almost forgot—my dog, Dawson, my buddy, my pal, my sidekick in life,
the one who truly listens and gets me.

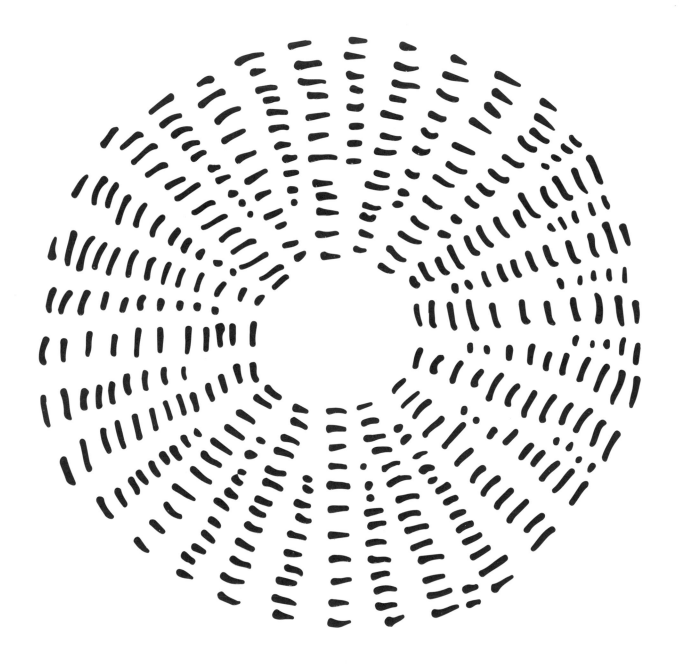

Contents

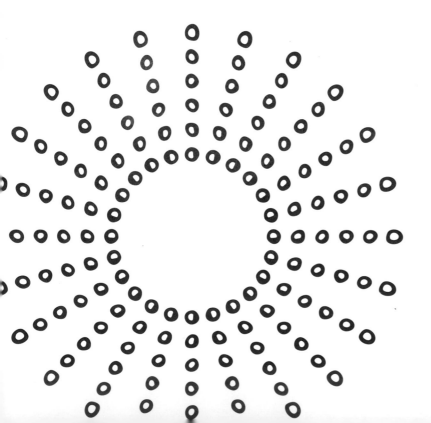

Introduction

The purpose of this journal is to inspire you to reach your goals—*any* goal—by writing it down. That's it! My big lofty plan is for you to put pen to paper. For now, I am not trying to solve world peace or have everyone agree politically and shake hands (maybe later), I just need you to take a few minutes everyday to clear your head and focus in on what you really want. There is a ton of evidence, which I will present to you as we go along, that proves you are way more likely to achieve your goals if you write them down. You will also create more positive thoughts about yourself. As I see it, there is no downside, and my only job is to provide a journal that (here it comes—my tagline and ultimate belief), will only take 1 to 3 minutes a day and allow you to change your body and your life in a positive way.

I want you to feel good about who you are right now, where you are right now, and then get excited about where you are going. I want you to look inside, at those darn emotions, and write down how you really feel, and admit what you want. Now you don't have to show anybody or share but you do have to be brutally honest with yourself. To get where we want to go, we have to know where we are now and love it or at least accept it.

My mission with this journal/guidebook is to gently nudge you (okay, sometimes push) in the direction I know you want to go. I want to help redirect your thoughts in a positive, focused manner so that you get what you're after and then some. A lighthearted, fun, easy, quick, uncomplicated way for you to write down your hopes and dreams and then see them come to life one page at a time.

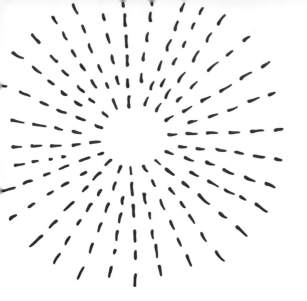

How to Use Your Journal

Ease and flow, baby. That is my motto and what we are after. When you start your first journal you will design your **G.A.M.E. Plan** for the first thirty days, which is already outlined for you, pick your **Power Statement** to keep you in the right mindset, and off you go. I also want you to sign a contract, so you stay true to your commitment to yourself and do a **Brain Drain**, to get rid of all that negative chatter.

At the beginning of each week there will be a theme to focus on, which will alternate between four topics: Mindset, Start a Movement, Food Freedom, and Spiritual Life Balance. Every day there will be a suggestion as to how you can stay focused on the area we are highlighting. Now, keep in mind, you are still working on your personal goal, but since we are all after mental and physical well-being I will give you fun things to jog your brain and keep on track. Again, these are suggestions, bonus tidbits to keep you motivated to reach your goals. I don't want you to get overwhelmed and feel you have to do all of them, but I do want you to give them a shot. I believe you should pick what feels good for you and build on it to fit your personality.

In between each week we will do a quick reset to see what's working and what you might want to change up. Those few deep breaths you take to get your next week ready will make things go a lot smoother.

In between the thirty-day journals we will do a **Big Picture Reset**. This is where you take a few more deep breaths and see how you did with your plan and reaching your goals. You can decide whether you want to stay with the same goal and area of life, or switch things up and move on. Remember, this is a no-judgment zone. If you hit your goals, awesome—celebrate, do the happy dance, milk it, and move on. But if you didn't and you had a few setbacks, shake if off, learn from it, and reset. I am just so proud of you for putting yourself out there and going after what you really want. So many people are afraid of the F-word (failure, *shhh*), that they don't reach for the stars—but not you, not this time. We are in it together and I've got your back.

Your Daily Journal

This will only take you 1 to 3 minutes a day, I promise.

The left side is the overall picture for the day, and the one you should complete every day, no matter what. On the right side we get more into your food and movement. This is on you to monitor and decide if it will help you to reach your goals. I've broken it into two components: Food Freedom and Start a Movement.

Food Freedom

I believe that to have an enjoyable and healthy life, we need to embrace food, feel great about what we eat, and be grateful for it. There is so much good and fresh food out there and millions of unique recipes to try. I choose to dwell on all of the awesome things that I can eat and enjoy. I am not a fan of diets or extreme plans that you can't stick with, but there are some pretty cool ways to kick-start your healthy habits. Pick a way that fits your personality and lifestyle and remember you can always switch it up. A couple favorite books:

- *The Whole30: The 30-Day Guide to Total Health and Food Freedom* by Melissa Hartwig and Dallas Hartwig
- *The Blood Sugar Solution 10-Day Detox Die*t by Mark Hyman

Those are not long-term plans, they are just meant to get you on the right path. The short-term plans will show you what it feels like to eat healthfully. The following are some long-term styles of eating that I think highly of and have seen people truly enjoy:

- Paleo/caveman-style
- Mediterranean diet
- Vegetarian/vegan
- Grain-free
- Gluten-free
- Sugar-free

The most important thing to remember with any food plan is to notice how it makes you *feel*. It's not about losing weight or dropping a dress size. There is something out there for everyone. How will you know which is right for you? The right eating style for your body and personality will be sure to put a pep in your step. Meeting with a health food coach would be the ultimate way to find out. If that's not possible, just remember to pick one that resonates with you and your body. In your Daily Journal there will be a space to write down what you ate and drank, as well as how you feel about your food. If you would like more suggestions or ideas to help you with your food plan please go to my website, www.sandyjoyweston.com.

Start a Movement

I just want you to move, five minutes here, five minutes there, five minutes anywhere. I want you to get up as often as possible and *move*. Walk around or dance around. I want you to clear your head as often as possible and move your body. I want you to see success and build on it. So, if you don't already have a fitness program that you've stuck with, then I want you to just do five minutes minimum a day. You can do more and that would be fab extra credit, but I want you to reach your goal, and feel great. Now, if you do have a workout program and you want to build on it and/or keep a bit more consistent, that is a different story and one I can get behind. Remember, pick a goal that is just slightly out of your reach and make sure you put your workouts in your calendar as if it is an appointment you can't miss. There are so many amazing fitness programs that you can do at home or at the gym—please, I beg of you to pick one you will look forward to (or hate the least). Whenever anyone asks me what the best workout is . . . I always say the same thing: "*The one you will do!*" Your Daily Journal will have a place for you to write down your workout or movement—seeing is believing.

If you want to try a new fitness program that you can do at home or on the road I did create a workout system called the ***H30 Workout***. The system is all about keeping you mentally in the game so that you can work out full-throttle with an "I can do this attitude." All the exercises are done in forty-five second intervals with fifteen second breaks. Every exercise is full-body, so you burn as many calories and hit as many muscles as possible. You don't even have to do the full 30 minutes if you are not there yet, that is the beauty of the system. It is for all levels and can be modified to fit your plan. You can find more details, workouts, and tips related to the *H30 Workout System* on my website, www.sandyjoyweston.com.

Ready, Set, Goal

Morning Prep. Start your day right. Before your feet hit the floor take a few seconds to think about what you want your day to look like, how are you going to show up in the world? What word could you focus on throughout the day to shift you into a positive mindset?

Before writing in your journal, reset your brain. Take three deep breaths, check off the boxes, and write down your word.

Write your **Power Statement** and your **Action Plan** as an everyday reminder—I'll explain these in a bit.

The other areas of your well-being you can rate on a scale of 1 to 10. Just mark how you felt you did that day: 1 being not so great and 10 meaning you rocked it. This does not have to be exact, it's just another visual aid to remind you of the areas that you want to develop for your mental and physical well-being. Some of the areas may not relate to your goal for this month, that's no problem, just focus on what you want and let these areas be a guide.

Some areas that may need further explanation are **Thoughts & Visualization** and **Meditation**. **Thoughts & Visualization** is about you being mindful of the thoughts you have about yourself and your goals. This is not for you to judge yourself, but to just acknowledge what is going on up there and see how you can shift those thoughts to be more positive. The same goes with visualization—the more you can truly see and feel your goals/dreams coming true the more they will happen. You don't need a big chunk of time, whenever you get a moment see yourself already accomplishing your goal/dream and let that joyful emotion take over your body. If possible, close your eyes and go through each and every incredible step.

As far as **Meditation**, if you have your own practice and want to build on it, that is awesome, but if not I would love for you to try just a minute here and there, throughout the day. I have included a section on fun little ways to reset your brain, that should give you a head start.

All these areas are for you to have a well-balanced plan, but you don't have to focus on them all. This is your personal plan and you should do the areas that resonate with you and your mission. A little bit every day can make a huge difference in your life.

Other Commonly Asked Questions:

Can I change my goal mid-month?
Yes, of course you can.

Can I go after more than one goal?
I am sure there are many things you've been wanting to go after, which is why you picked up this journal, but let's just pick one big goal for now and I promise you, the rest will fall in place. I want you to see success.

Can I change my Power Statement before the month is up?
Yes, you can keep redefining it so it motivates you.

Can I start my journal mid-month, or mid-week?
Yes, that is why the days and months are there for you to fill in. I want to break that mindset that you have to wait for the beginning of the month or week to get back on track. You can have a *do-over* whenever you decide.

I hope that answers a few of your questions. I'm sure there will be more and I am here to help, so feel free to go to my website, www.sandyjoyweston. com, and ask away.

The Philosophy

Every great coach tells their athletes that victory comes first in the head, then on the playing field. Every champion first visualizes crossing the finish line, making the basket, or scoring the goal before lifting the trophy in reality. This type of focus and mental training is the prime ingredient in every athletic accomplishment. Why can't each and every one of us apply this to our own lives?

G.A.M.E. stands for Goals, Action, Motivation, Energy! Achieving your fitness goals first starts with resetting your brain, clearing your head to gain focus, and then igniting the power that is deep inside you.

The G.A.M.E. Plan is about goal-getting. It is about achieving your goals and believing with every part of your brain and body that you will get there. It is also about having fun along the way!

After many years of research, I've broken down the complex theories developed by professional coaches, positive psychologists, athletes, scientists, and trainers, and I delivered them in a program that is highly effective and easy to follow. The G.A.M.E. Plan focuses on what you can do right now and what you will accomplish in a very short period of time.

If you need some extra motivation, psychology professor Dr. Gail Matthews at the Dominican University in California did a study showing that you are 42 percent more likely to reach your goals if you write them down. It makes sense, doesn't it? If you look at what you want every day and think about it over and over again, there is no way you won't plan out your day differently and jog that brain of yours to stay on track.

What's Your G.A.M.E. Plan?

Goal

What do you want?

_____

_____

Action

What will you do the get there?

_____

_____

Motivation

Why are you really doing this?

_____

_____

Energy

How are you feeling today?

_____

_____

All it takes is 1 to 3 minutes a day to change your body and your life in a positive way!

"G"—Goals for Success

Setting realistic goals and seeing results is what it's all about. I want you to reach your goals and have fun. There are three key components to goal setting: have clear targets, be persistent, and find out what you really like to do.

To set a clear target you want to be able to feel it, touch it, see it, and yes, smell it. You want to use all your senses to experience your goal as if it is already happening. I highly suggest picking a goal that is just slightly out of reach. We want to see success and build on it. Many people get discouraged because they go after something that is extreme from where they are right now. I get it, you want instant gratification, but what I want for you is to feel joy. I want you to enjoy the process *and* reach your goals.

To be persistent means you can get knocked down a few times, and get back up and go after what you came here for. Remember, there is no failure. Failure would be not trying, and you are more than trying. So if it doesn't go perfectly, who cares, this is your life and you are worth every do-over and then some.

Lastly, finding out what you really like to do will make your experience fun, as well as rewarding.

Examples of Goals:

1. I want to look better in my clothes.
2. I want to feel great while playing with the kids.
3. I want to lose 15 pounds.
4. I want to run a 5k.
5. I want to eat healthy.
6. I want to feel mentally and physically strong.
7. I want to develop more muscle tone.
8. I want to lose inches and drop body fat.
9. I want to build muscle.
10. I want to buy new clothes.

Bonus Ones for Life:

1. I want a new home.
2. I want to perform in front of people.
3. I want new friends.
4. I want a significant other.
5. I want new roommates.

"A"—Action Plan

What are you willing to do to meet your goal? These are all suggestions, but feel free to make up one of your own. It has to feel exciting to you. Make sure to be as specific as possible.

If you are not ready to do the **Action** it will take to reach your goal, then go back and change your goal. You really want to think about your days as if you are going to carve out the time to get what you want. You must put it in, as if it is an appointment you *cannot* cancel.

1. I enjoy taking a _____ minute walk at lunch ___x a week.
2. I look forward to lifting weights ___x a week.
3. It's awesome to hike/walk with my dog ___x a week.
4. I dance around my house _____ minutes a day to my favorite tunes.
5. I love taking fitness classes with my friends ___x a week.
6. I get more workouts in while doing my chores—stairs, lunges, squats, push-ups, etc.
7. I train for my upcoming race ___x a week for _____ minutes.
8. I bike ride with friends ___x a week for _____ minutes.
9. I workout at home ___x a week for _____ minutes.
10. I enjoy going to dance classes ___x a week.
11. Cooking healthy meals ___x a week is very enjoyable.
12. Grocery shopping and planning my meals for the week is very rewarding.

Okay, I think you get the idea. Now just in case you want to apply this to other parts of your life, it works for all areas, here are some examples:

1. I enjoy going out on a date ___x a week.
2. Meeting my friends out ___x a week is so much fun.
3. Budgeting my money every week is very freeing.
4. Calling ___x amount of people every week for my new business is so rewarding.
5. Applying for ___x amount of jobs is invigorating.
6. Cleaning out one room in my home ___x per week is such a good feeling.

"M"—Motivation

Let's be real—why do you really want this goal? What is the under-lying reason for your motivation? Your motivation is what is going to keep you in the game when you want to give up. It's important to tap into your motivation in a positive way, and knowing this, you can pick a **Power Statement.**

Here are some examples:

1. I got divorced and need to get back in the game.
2. I want to go out more.
3. I want to run a 5k.
4. I want to be healthy for my kids.
5. I want a significant other in my life.
6. I want to feel sexy.
7. I want to look great for my reunion.
8. I want to look good in my bikini when I go on vacation.
9. I want to feel good when I look in the mirror.
10. I want to love my body.

"E"—Energy

As individuals we have different ways that we show how we feel. Some people are known to have high energy and others are just mellow and go at a slower pace. Here, I am thinking of your energy level each day as your overall well-being. How are you feeling today, mentally and physically? I don't want you to just get by or feel good, I want you to aim much higher, feel amazing, joyful, even incredible! I realize that this is not possible every day but I do want it to be *most* days and that is why I want you to rate how you feel on a scale of 1 to 10 daily—10 is the best it gets and 1 is, well, better days to come. This is just for you to be aware of how you are feeling so you can make changes and find solutions for your beautiful, amazing life.

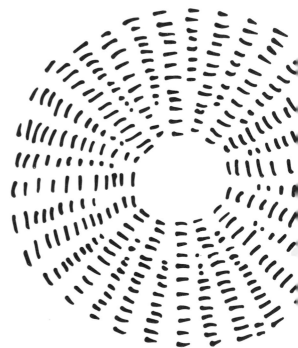

Power Statements

Your Power Statement focuses you everyday on truly being in the moment. This statement tells a story, the story of why you are here. The *why* is a reminder so that you are determined to get through the *how*—your Action Plan. Your "why" needs to be so big that the "how" pales in comparison.

Power Statements should always be said in the present moment, as if they are happening right now. Saying them as if they are going to happen pushes them off to that imaginary day. Let's take responsibility for now and take this first little step which leads us to the next step which leads us to accomplishing what we set out to do. Pick a Power Statement that you aspire to achieve, and feels slightly out of your reach—make it something that draws out the passion in you. Your Power Statement should correlate with your G.A.M.E. Plan.

You will be writing your Power Statement every day so don't make it too long, and make sure when you say it out loud it makes you feel good. Here are a few ideas, but feel free to create your own.

1. I like the way I look and feel.
2. I am strong and powerful.
3. I eat to feel good inside and out.
4. I eat meals that make me feel great.
5. Working out is so much fun.
6. I feel wonderful today.
7. It feels awesome to get a good night's sleep.
8. I enjoy going to my new gym.
9. I really look forward to my bike club.
10. Running in the morning makes me happy.
11. Meditating makes my days ease and flow.
12. I love the way I look in my clothes.
13. I am sexy and beautiful.

Now it is time for those bonus ones you can apply to the other parts of your life.

1. I have so much fun on my dates.
2. I love hanging out with my new friends.
3. I just love being in my home.
4. Financial freedom feels so good.
5. I am very passionate about my job.
6. I find joy in each and every day.
7. My business is kicking butt and is so much fun.
8. My new apartment is great to entertain in.

Brain Drain

This is your chance! We all have negative chatter. Get it out of your head and leave it here, where it belongs.

Here are some examples:

1. I've been this weight my whole life. What's the point in changing now?
2. I'm not worthy of feeling good or looking great.
3. It will take too much time to work out and eat healthy.
4. I'm too busy for all of this.
5. Who could love someone like me?
6. Working out is too hard and it hurts too much.
7. I hate eating healthy.
8. I'm too old to get in shape now.

Here are some bonus life thoughts to get out and stomp out:

1. I am too busy at work to do anything else.
2. I have a family, no time for me.
3. I have responsibilities, no time for fun.
4. I can't afford to go out.
5. I will never make enough money.
6. I will never have time to travel.
7. Who has time to meditate?
8. No one will ever appreciate me.
9. I am going to be lonely forever.
10. I am too shy to perform.

Wow, those were pretty negative, glad we are done with that section. Ouch! When you are done writing out your own negative chatter, put a big X through them—be gone.

Scribble Scrabble

This is your space to write your thoughts, good or bad. You can also use it for extra space to remind yourself of stuff you want to do. You can doodle, decorate, write quotes, make a poem, write a love letter, or paste a sticker in the space. Whatever you feel that day, have at it.

Scribble Scrabble is so fun and freeing. Here are a few examples of what you could put in the space. Remember there is no right or wrong, and these are just suggestions.

Man, did I blow that workout. I can't believe I let the time get away from me. Tomorrow I will schedule it in.

I'm so glad I took the time to go meet up with my friends for dinner. I deserved it!

Sample Journal Pages

Food Freedom

Plan: Mediterranean

Meal One: Smoothie: protein powder, kale, spinach, apple, lime, turmeric.

Meal Two: Bowl of Portuguese Kale Sausage Soup at Gryphon's café.

Meal Three: Large veggie salad with chicken and bacon. Oil and balsamic vinegar dressing.

Snacks: 1/4 cup of hummus with blue corn chips.

Beverages: 6 (8-oz.) glasses of water, 2 cups of coffee with oat milk.

Start a Movement
30-minute workout at home
30-minute walk with dog

How did you feel about your food today?

How did you feel about your workout today?

Feel satisfied?
1 ———————————————— 10

Enjoy your food?
1 ———————————————— 10

Eat slow / seated?
1 ———————————————— 10

Stick to the plan?
1 ———————————————— 10

Did you enjoy it?
1 ———————————————— 10

Do you feel energized?
1 ———————————————— 10

Overall energy: 8

Sample Journal Pages

Date: Monday, Jan. 1st!

Power Statement: I eat and move to look and feel amazing.

Action Plan: Meditate every morning and night for 5 minutes, lift weights 3x a week & cook 2x a week.

Morning Prep ✓

3 Deep Breaths ✓

Word of the Day: Joy

Daily Focus:

Today I want to focus on one word that makes me smile—Joy.

Thoughts & Visualization

1 —————————————— 10

Food / Water

1 —————————————— 10

Daily Movement / Workout

1 —————————————— 10

Sleep

1 —————————————— 10

Meditation

1 —————————————— 10

Scribble Scrabble

I am:

- Joyful
- Fun
- Accepting
- Great friend
- Awesome mom

Reset Your G.A.M.E. Plan
Samples

What can you build on?
Having more healthy food in the house.

What worked last week?
It really helped to meditate in the morning and prep my food.

Planner
Go to the grocery store Sunday & Wednesday.
Try a new class at the gym 3x a week.
Don't answer emails after 8:00 p.m.

Big Picture Reset
Samples

What positive habits did you form the last 30 days?

I meditated in the morning, cooked once a week, & lifted weights 3x a week.

How could you adjust your schedule to fit your G.A.M.E. Plan?

1. Go to bed an hour earlier.
2. Cook once a week with my husband.
3. Go grocery shopping with my friend.

How could you shift your mindset to reach your new G.A.M.E. Plan?

Try to write down more of my dreams rather than sharing with people before I am totally ready to go forth and conquer. I don't need to hear how the odds are stacked against me.

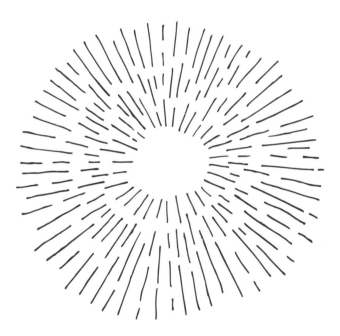

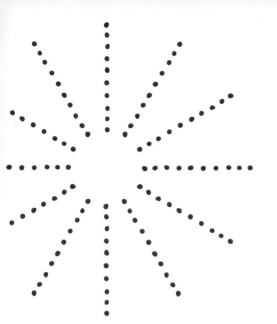

Your First 30 Days Start Now!

What's Your G.A.M.E. Plan?

Goal

What do you want?

_____

_____

Action

What will you do the get there?

_____

_____

Motivation

Why are you really doing this?

_____

_____

Energy

How are you feeling today?

_____

_____

All it takes is 1 to 3 minutes a day to change your body and your life in a positive way!

Brain Drain

Squash those negative buggers!

Contract

I, _____, am not responsible for my pre-existing thoughts. I am only aware of them. From this day forward, I now accept who I am, how I think and what I think, and I fully embrace the idea that I can change all of these things, one word at a time. And that's awesome.

If I accept this challenge, I will set realistic goals, whether it's to run a triathlon or get my butt off the sofa for just twenty minutes. I will train my brain like an athlete. I will focus my thoughts and move my body to achieve my full potential. I will succeed because it will be a blast.

Signature: _____ Date: _____

Pre-Game

Week: 1

Theme: Mindset

This week it is about the little things you can do to shift your thoughts to highlight all the positives in your life. It is so easy to focus on the areas of your life that aren't going so well, which we all have the tendency to do. By thinking of all the stuff that is going great, the other stuff will come along for the ride.

Scribble Scrabble:

"Once we believe in ourselves, we can risk curiosity, wonder, spontaneous delight, or any experience that reveals the human spirit." —e. e. cummings

Date:

Power Statement:

Action Plan:

Morning Prep ◯

3 Deep Breaths ◯

Word of the Day:

Thoughts & Visualization

1 _____ 10

Food / Water

1 _____ 10

Daily Movement / Workout

1 _____ 10

Sleep

1 _____ 10

Meditation

1 _____ 10

Daily Focus:

Today, focus on one word that makes you smile (example: Joy).

Scribble Scrabble:

Date:

Mindset

Plan:

Meal One:

Meal Two:

Meal Three:

Snacks:

Beverages:

Start a Movement!

How did you feel about your food today?

How did you feel about your workout today?

Feel satisfied?

1 _____ 10

Enjoy your food?

1 _____ 10

Eat slow / seated?

1 _____ 10

Stick to the plan?

1 _____ 10

Did you enjoy it?

1 _____ 10

Do you feel energized?

1 _____ 10

Overall energy:

> *"The mind is the limit. As long as the mind can envision the fact that you can do something, you can do it, as long as you really believe 100 percent."* —Arnold Schwarzenegger

Date:

Power Statement:

Action Plan:

Morning Prep ◯

3 Deep Breaths ◯

Word of the Day:

Thoughts & Visualization

1 _____ 10

Food / Water

1 _____ 10

Daily Movement / Workout

1 _____ 10

Sleep

1 _____ 10

Meditation

1 _____ 10

Daily Focus:

Today, think of 5 things that make you smile.

Scribble Scrabble:

Week: 1

Date:

Mindset

Plan:

Meal One:

Meal Two:

Meal Three:

Snacks:

Beverages:

Start a Movement!

How did you feel about your food today?

How did you feel about your workout today?

Feel satisfied?

1 _____ 10

Did you enjoy it?

1 _____ 10

Enjoy your food?

1 _____ 10

Do you feel energized?

1 _____ 10

Eat slow / seated?

1 _____ 10

Stick to the plan?

1 _____ 10

Overall energy:

Week: 1

"It doesn't hurt to ask. There is no downside to asking. Dream big, go big. You will be shocked at the yeses you get." —Sandy Joy Weston

Date:

Power Statement:

Action Plan:

Morning Prep ◯

3 Deep Breaths ◯

Word of the Day:

Thoughts & Visualization

1 _____ 10

Food / Water

1 _____ 10

Daily Movement / Workout

1 _____ 10

Sleep

1 _____ 10

Meditation

1 _____ 10

Daily Focus:

Think of 5 things that you like about yourself.

Scribble Scrabble:

Week: 1

Date:

Mindset

Plan:

Meal One:

Meal Two:

Meal Three:

Snacks:

Beverages:

Start a Movement!

How did you feel about your food today?

How did you feel about your workout today?

Feel satisfied?

1 _____ 10

Enjoy your food?

1 _____ 10

Eat slow / seated?

1 _____ 10

Stick to the plan?

1 _____ 10

Did you enjoy it?

1 _____ 10

Do you feel energized?

1 _____ 10

Overall energy:

Week: 1

"Gold medals aren't really made of gold. They're made of sweat, determination, and a hard-to-find alloy called guts." —Dan Gable

Date:

Power Statement:

Action Plan:

Morning Prep ◯

3 Deep Breaths ◯

Word of the Day:

Thoughts & Visualization

1 _____ 10

Food / Water

1 _____ 10

Daily Movement / Workout

1 _____ 10

Sleep

1 _____ 10

Meditation

1 _____ 10

Daily Focus:

Think of 1 thing you like about your body.

Scribble Scrabble:

Date:

Mindset

Plan:

Meal One:

Meal Two:

Meal Three:

Snacks:

Beverages:

Start a Movement!

How did you feel about your food today?

How did you feel about your workout today?

Feel satisfied?

1 _____ 10

Did you enjoy it?

1 _____ 10

Enjoy your food?

1 _____ 10

Do you feel energized?

1 _____ 10

Eat slow / seated?

1 _____ 10

Stick to the plan?

1 _____ 10

Overall energy:

Week: 1

"There is always sunshine amongst the clouds. Sometimes you just have to look a little deeper. If you squint real hard, you can see the light even on the darkest days." —Sandy Joy Weston

Date:

Power Statement:

Action Plan:

Morning Prep ◯

3 Deep Breaths ◯

Word of the Day:

Thoughts & Visualization

1 _____ 10

Food / Water

1 _____ 10

Daily Movement / Workout

1 _____ 10

Sleep

1 _____ 10

Meditation

1 _____ 10

Daily Focus:

Think of your motivation to be healthy.

Scribble Scrabble:

Week: 1

Date:

Mindset

Plan:

Meal One:

Meal Two:

Meal Three:

Snacks:

Beverages:

Start a Movement!

How did you feel about your food today?

How did you feel about your workout today?

Feel satisfied?

1 _____ 10

Did you enjoy it?

1 _____ 10

Enjoy your food?

1 _____ 10

Do you feel energized?

1 _____ 10

Eat slow / seated?

1 _____ 10

Stick to the plan?

1 _____ 10

Overall energy:

Week: 1

"Courage is resistance to fear, mastery of fear—not absence of fear." —Mark Twain

Date:

Power Statement:

Action Plan:

Morning Prep ◯

3 Deep Breaths ◯

Word of the Day:

Thoughts & Visualization

1 _____ 10

Food / Water

1 _____ 10

Daily Movement / Workout

1 _____ 10

Sleep

1 _____ 10

Meditation

1 _____ 10

Daily Focus:

Today, I want you to look in the mirror and say "I love you."

Scribble Scrabble:

Week: 1

Date:

Mindset

Plan:

Meal One:

Meal Two:

Meal Three:

Snacks:

Beverages:

Start a Movement!

How did you feel about your food today?

How did you feel about your workout today?

Feel satisfied?

1 _____ 10

Enjoy your food?

1 _____ 10

Eat slow / seated?

1 _____ 10

Stick to the plan?

1 _____ 10

Did you enjoy it?

1 _____ 10

Do you feel energized?

1 _____ 10

Overall energy:

"No matter what life puts you through, even when some things are truly sad, there is always love in every direction surrounding you." —Sandy Joy Weston

Date:

Power Statement:

Action Plan:

Morning Prep ○

3 Deep Breaths ○

Word of the Day:

Thoughts & Visualization

1 _____ 10

Food / Water

1 _____ 10

Daily Movement / Workout

1 _____ 10

Sleep

1 _____ 10

Meditation

1 _____ 10

Daily Focus:

Remind yourself of why you want to feel and look great.

Scribble Scrabble:

Week: 1

Date:

Mindset

Plan:

Meal One:

Start a Movement!

Meal Two:

Meal Three:

Snacks:

Beverages:

How did you feel about your food today?

How did you feel about your workout today?

Feel satisfied?

1 _____ 10

Did you enjoy it?

1 _____ 10

Enjoy your food?

1 _____ 10

Do you feel energized?

1 _____ 10

Eat slow / seated?

1 _____ 10

Stick to the plan?

1 _____ 10

Overall energy:

Week: 1

Reset Your Head

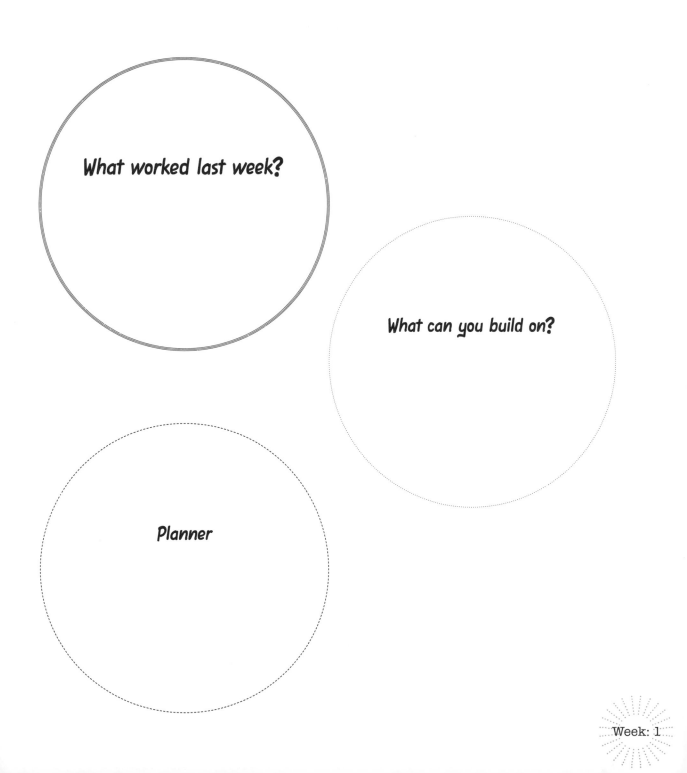

What worked last week?

What can you build on?

Planner

Week: 1

Pre-Game

Week: 2

Theme: Food Freedom

This week we are going to work on why, when, where, and how you eat. We want to eat to fuel our souls and to feel satisfied and joyful—not when we are sad, rewarding ourselves, or using food as a coping mechanism. Let's keep it real with where we are so we can get to where we want to go—fun with food.

Scribble Scrabble:

"Never throw in the towel. Go until the very end and you will succeed."
—Sandy Joy Weston

Date:

Power Statement:

Action Plan:

Morning Prep ◯

3 Deep Breaths ◯

Word of the Day:

Thoughts & Visualization

1 _____ 10

Food / Water

1 _____ 10

Daily Movement / Workout

1 _____ 10

Sleep

1 _____ 10

Meditation

1 _____ 10

Daily Focus:

Be aware of what and when you are eating.

Scribble Scrabble:

Week: 2

Date:

Food Freedom

Plan:

Meal One:

Meal Two:

Meal Three:

Snacks:

Beverages:

Start a Movement!

How did you feel about your food today?

How did you feel about your workout today?

Feel satisfied?

1 _____ 10

Enjoy your food?

1 _____ 10

Eat slow / seated?

1 _____ 10

Stick to the plan?

1 _____ 10

Did you enjoy it?

1 _____ 10

Do you feel energized?

1 _____ 10

Overall energy:

"Most people never run far enough on their first wind to find out they've got a second."
—William James

Date:

Power Statement:

Action Plan:

Morning Prep	◯
3 Deep Breaths	◯
Word of the Day:	

Thoughts & Visualization

1 _____ 10

Food / Water

1 _____ 10

Daily Movement / Workout

1 _____ 10

Sleep

1 _____ 10

Meditation

1 _____ 10

Daily Focus:

Today I only want you to eat sitting down.

Scribble Scrabble:

Date:

Food Freedom

Plan:

Meal One:

Meal Two:

Meal Three:

Snacks:

Beverages:

Start a Movement!

How did you feel about your food today?

How did you feel about your workout today?

Feel satisfied?

1 _____ 10

Did you enjoy it?

1 _____ 10

Enjoy your food?

1 _____ 10

Do you feel energized?

1 _____ 10

Eat slow / seated?

1 _____ 10

Stick to the plan?

1 _____ 10

Overall energy:

Week: 2

"Every moment is a fresh beginning." —T. S. Eliot

Date:

Power Statement:

Action Plan:

| Morning Prep ◯ |
| 3 Deep Breaths ◯ |
| Word of the Day: |

Thoughts & Visualization

1 _____ 10

Food / Water

1 _____ 10

Daily Movement / Workout

1 _____ 10

Sleep

1 _____ 10

Meditation

1 _____ 10

Daily Focus:

Today I want you to eat slowly and until you are satisfied.

Scribble Scrabble:

Week: 2

Date:

Food Freedom

Plan:

Meal One:

Meal Two:

Meal Three:

Snacks:

Beverages:

Start a Movement!

How did you feel about your food today?

How did you feel about your workout today?

Feel satisfied?

1 _____ 10

Did you enjoy it?

1 _____ 10

Enjoy your food?

1 _____ 10

Do you feel energized?

1 _____ 10

Eat slow / seated?

1 _____ 10

Stick to the plan?

1 _____ 10

Overall energy:

"Your brain is like any other muscle, you can train and condition it so you feel more emotions that serve you well. The more you imagine joy the more joy there will be in your life." —Sandy Joy Weston

Date:

Power Statement:

Action Plan:

Morning Prep ○

3 Deep Breaths ○

Word of the Day:

Thoughts & Visualization

1 _____ 10

Food / Water

1 _____ 10

Daily Movement / Workout

1 _____ 10

Sleep

1 _____ 10

Meditation

1 _____ 10

Daily Focus:

Today I want you to take note of why you eat (no judgment).

Scribble Scrabble:

Date:

Food Freedom

Plan:

Meal One:

Meal Two:

Meal Three:

Snacks:

Beverages:

Start a Movement!

How did you feel about your food today?

How did you feel about your workout today?

Feel satisfied?

1 _____ 10

Did you enjoy it?

1 _____ 10

Enjoy your food?

1 _____ 10

Do you feel energized?

1 _____ 10

Eat slow / seated?

1 _____ 10

Stick to the plan?

1 _____ 10

Overall energy:

"Believe and act as if it were impossible to fail." —Charles F. Kettering

Date:

Power Statement:

Action Plan:

Morning Prep ◯

3 Deep Breaths ◯

Word of the Day:

```
       Thoughts & Visualization
1 _____ 10
```

Daily Focus:

Today I want you to eat only when you are hungry and really looking forward to it.

```
            Food / Water
1 _____ 10
```

```
    Daily Movement / Workout
1 _____ 10
```

```
               Sleep
1 _____ 10
```

```
            Meditation
1 _____ 10
```

Scribble Scrabble:

Date:

Food Freedom

Plan:

Meal One:

Meal Two:

Meal Three:

Snacks:

Beverages:

Start a Movement!

How did you feel about your food today?

How did you feel about your workout today?

Feel satisfied?

1 _____ 10

Did you enjoy it?

1 _____ 10

Enjoy your food?

1 _____ 10

Do you feel energized?

1 _____ 10

Eat slow / seated?

1 _____ 10

Stick to the plan?

1 _____ 10

Overall energy:

"Don't count the days, make the days count." —Muhammad Ali

Date:

Power Statement:

Action Plan:

Morning Prep ○

3 Deep Breaths ○

Word of the Day:

Thoughts & Visualization
1 _____ 10

Food / Water
1 _____ 10

Daily Movement / Workout
1 _____ 10

Sleep
1 _____ 10

Meditation
1 _____ 10

Daily Focus:

Today I want you to prepare a meal that is healthy and easy; set it up on a nice plate.

Scribble Scrabble:

Date:

Food Freedom

Plan:

Meal One:

Meal Two:

Meal Three:

Snacks:

Beverages:

Start a Movement!

How did you feel about your food today?

How did you feel about your workout today?

Feel satisfied?

1 _____ 10

Enjoy your food?

1 _____ 10

Eat slow / seated?

1 _____ 10

Stick to the plan?

1 _____ 10

Did you enjoy it?

1 _____ 10

Do you feel energized?

1 _____ 10

Overall energy:

> **"When you're in the right positive mindset, everything in your day will be perfectly timed." —Sandy Joy Weston**

Date:

Power Statement:

Action Plan:

Morning Prep ○

3 Deep Breaths ○

Word of the Day:

Thoughts & Visualization

1 _____ 10

Food / Water

1 _____ 10

Daily Movement / Workout

1 _____ 10

Sleep

1 _____ 10

Meditation

1 _____ 10

Daily Focus:

Make a list of all the amazing foods you enjoy eating that are good for you.

Scribble Scrabble:

Date:

Food Freedom

Plan:

Meal One:

Meal Two:

Meal Three:

Snacks:

Beverages:

Start a Movement!

How did you feel about your food today?

How did you feel about your workout today?

Feel satisfied?

1 _____ 10

Did you enjoy it?

1 _____ 10

Enjoy your food?

1 _____ 10

Do you feel energized?

1 _____ 10

Eat slow / seated?

1 _____ 10

Stick to the plan?

1 _____ 10

Overall energy:

Reset Your Head

What worked last week?

What can you build on?

Planner

Pre-Game

Week: 3

Theme: Spiritual Life Balance

This week I want to introduce you to little things that will help you connect to your inner/higher power. Give it a shot, it is worth the joy.

Scribble Scrabble:

"You happen to life. You choose your path. It is wide open. Love all of it, enjoy every bit." —Sandy Joy Weston

Date:

Power Statement:

Action Plan:

Morning Prep ◯

3 Deep Breaths ◯

Word of the Day:

Thoughts & Visualization

1 _____ 10

Food / Water

1 _____ 10

Daily Movement / Workout

1 _____ 10

Sleep

1 _____ 10

Meditation

1 _____ 10

Daily Focus:

Think of 5 things you appreciate in your life.

Scribble Scrabble:

Week: 3

Date:

Spiritual Life Balance

> **Plan:**

Meal One:

Meal Two:

Meal Three:

Snacks:

Beverages:

> **Start a Movement!**

> How did you feel about your food today?

> How did you feel about your workout today?

Feel satisfied?

1 _____ 10

Did you enjoy it?

1 _____ 10

Enjoy your food?

1 _____ 10

Do you feel energized?

1 _____ 10

Eat slow / seated?

1 _____ 10

Stick to the plan?

1 _____ 10

Overall energy: ◯

"The journey of a thousand miles begins with a single step." —Lao Tzu

Date:

Power Statement:

Action Plan:

Morning Prep ○

3 Deep Breaths ○

Word of the Day:

Thoughts & Visualization

1 _____ 10

Food / Water

1 _____ 10

Daily Movement / Workout

1 _____ 10

Sleep

1 _____ 10

Meditation

1 _____ 10

Daily Focus:

Today when you get stressed, take 4 deep breaths in and out and reconnect.

Scribble Scrabble:

Date:

Spiritual Life Balance

Plan:

Meal One:

Meal Two:

Meal Three:

Snacks:

Beverages:

Start a Movement!

How did you feel about your food today?

How did you feel about your workout today?

Feel satisfied?

1 _____ 10

Did you enjoy it?

1 _____ 10

Enjoy your food?

1 _____ 10

Do you feel energized?

1 _____ 10

Eat slow / seated?

1 _____ 10

Stick to the plan?

1 _____ 10

Overall energy:

Week: 3

"Sometimes you win, and sometimes you don't, but if you go into it with strength in your true self, then you will win every time." —Sandy Joy Weston

Date:

Power Statement:

Action Plan:

Morning Prep ◯

3 Deep Breaths ◯

Word of the Day:

Thoughts & Visualization

1 _____ 10

Food / Water

1 _____ 10

Daily Movement / Workout

1 _____ 10

Sleep

1 _____ 10

Meditation

1 _____ 10

Daily Focus:

Before your feet hit the floor, take 1 minute to breathe and think of a positive word.

Scribble Scrabble:

Week: 3

Date:

Spiritual Life Balance

Plan:

Meal One:

Meal Two:

Meal Three:

Snacks:

Beverages:

Start a Movement!

How did you feel about your food today?

How did you feel about your workout today?

Feel satisfied?

1 _____ 10

Did you enjoy it?

1 _____ 10

Enjoy your food?

1 _____ 10

Do you feel energized?

1 _____ 10

Eat slow / seated?

1 _____ 10

Stick to the plan?

1 _____ 10

Overall energy:

"Tough times never last, but tough people do." —Dr. Robert Schuller

Date:

Power Statement:

Action Plan:

Morning Prep ◯

3 Deep Breaths ◯

Word of the Day:

Thoughts & Visualization

1 _____ 10

Food / Water

1 _____ 10

Daily Movement / Workout

1 _____ 10

Sleep

1 _____ 10

Meditation

1 _____ 10

Daily Focus:

Remind yourself that you are worthy of all life's joys.

Scribble Scrabble:

Date:

Spiritual Life Balance

Plan:

Meal One:

Meal Two:

Meal Three:

Snacks:

Beverages:

Start a Movement!

How did you feel about your food today?

How did you feel about your workout today?

Feel satisfied?

1 _____ 10

Did you enjoy it?

1 _____ 10

Enjoy your food?

1 _____ 10

Do you feel energized?

1 _____ 10

Eat slow / seated?

1 _____ 10

Stick to the plan?

1 _____ 10

Overall energy:

Week: 3

"You may get shut down and you may get censored, but you still need to speak from your heart, stand tall, and stand bold. True power comes from one person connected to their true self." —Sandy Joy Weston

Date:

Power Statement:

Action Plan:

Morning Prep ○

3 Deep Breaths ○

Word of the Day:

Thoughts & Visualization

1 _____ 10

Food / Water

1 _____ 10

Daily Movement / Workout

1 _____ 10

Sleep

1 _____ 10

Meditation

1 _____ 10

Daily Focus:

Tonight I want you to meditate a few minutes before bed.

Scribble Scrabble:

Date:

Spiritual Life Balance

Plan:

Meal One:

Meal Two:

Meal Three:

Snacks:

Beverages:

Start a Movement!

How did you feel about your food today?

How did you feel about your workout today?

Feel satisfied?

1 _____ 10

Enjoy your food?

1 _____ 10

Eat slow / seated?

1 _____ 10

Stick to the plan?

1 _____ 10

Did you enjoy it?

1 _____ 10

Do you feel energized?

1 _____ 10

Overall energy:

Week: 3

"There is only one success: to be able to spend your life in your own way."
—Christopher Morley

Date:

Power Statement:

Action Plan:

Morning Prep ◯

3 Deep Breaths ◯

Word of the Day:

Thoughts & Visualization

1 _____ 10

Food / Water

1 _____ 10

Daily Movement / Workout

1 _____ 10

Sleep

1 _____ 10

Meditation

1 _____ 10

Daily Focus:

Today send love to 5 people who could use the extra care.

Scribble Scrabble:

Week: 3

Date:

Spiritual Life Balance

Plan:

Meal One:

Meal Two:

Meal Three:

Snacks:

Beverages:

Start a Movement!

How did you feel about your food today?

How did you feel about your workout today?

Feel satisfied?

1 _____ 10

Enjoy your food?

1 _____ 10

Eat slow / seated?

1 _____ 10

Stick to the plan?

1 _____ 10

Did you enjoy it?

1 _____ 10

Do you feel energized?

1 _____ 10

Overall energy: ◯

> **"If you are authentic to yourself, truly connected, you will always come from love." —Sandy Joy Weston**

Date:

Power Statement:

Action Plan:

Morning Prep ◯

3 Deep Breaths ◯

Word of the Day:

Thoughts & Visualization

1 _____ 10

Food / Water

1 _____ 10

Daily Movement / Workout

1 _____ 10

Sleep

1 _____ 10

Meditation

1 _____ 10

Daily Focus:

Tonight I want you to think of how you could change your routine to get 7–8 hours of sleep.

Scribble Scrabble:

Date:

Spiritual Life Balance

Plan:

Meal One:

Meal Two:

Meal Three:

Snacks:

Beverages:

Start a Movement!

How did you feel about your food today?

How did you feel about your workout today?

Feel satisfied?

1 _____ 10

Did you enjoy it?

1 _____ 10

Enjoy your food?

1 _____ 10

Do you feel energized?

1 _____ 10

Eat slow / seated?

1 _____ 10

Stick to the plan?

1 _____ 10

Overall energy: ◯

Week: 3

Reset Your Head

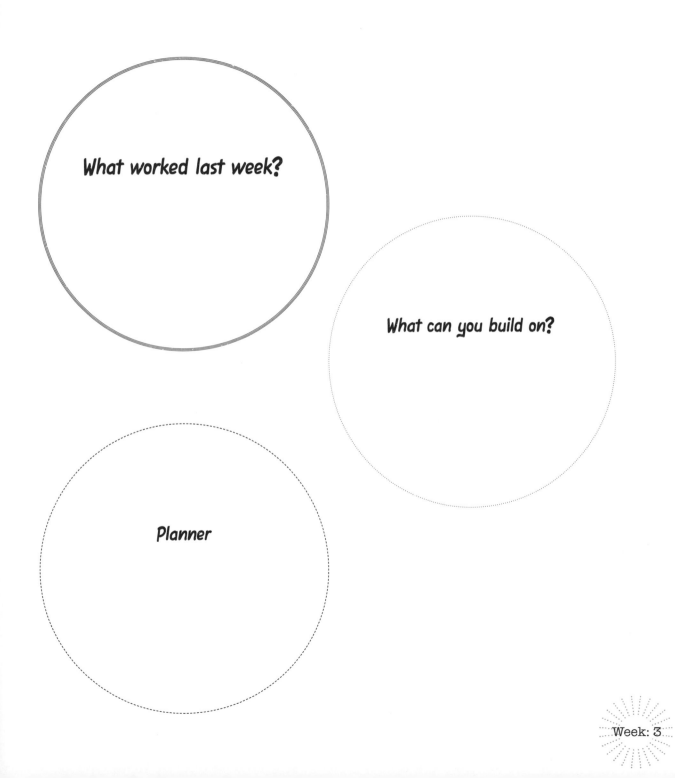

What worked last week?

What can you build on?

Planner

Week: 3

Pre-Game

Week: 4

Theme: Start a Movement

This week we are going to discover all the fun ways you like to move and work out. Let's try a bit of everything to see what floats your boat.

Scribble Scrabble:

"Light tomorrow with today." —Elizabeth Barrett Browning

Date:

Power Statement:

Action Plan:

Morning Prep ◯

3 Deep Breaths ◯

Word of the Day:

Thoughts & Visualization

1 _____ 10

Food / Water

1 _____ 10

Daily Movement / Workout

1 _____ 10

Sleep

1 _____ 10

Meditation

1 _____ 10

Daily Focus:

Today I want you to move 5 more minutes than your normal routine.

Scribble Scrabble:

Date:

Start a Movement

Plan:

Meal One:

Meal Two:

Meal Three:

Snacks:

Beverages:

Start a Movement!

How did you feel about your food today?

How did you feel about your workout today?

Feel satisfied?

1 _____ 10

Did you enjoy it?

1 _____ 10

Enjoy your food?

1 _____ 10

Do you feel energized?

1 _____ 10

Eat slow / seated?

1 _____ 10

Stick to the plan?

1 _____ 10

Overall energy:

"When your head's in a fog, just get up and move for one minute. Just one minute, and I promise you that everything will seem clearer." —Sandy Joy Weston

Date:

Power Statement:

Action Plan:

Morning Prep ○

3 Deep Breaths ○

Word of the Day:

Thoughts & Visualization

1 _____ 10

Food / Water

1 _____ 10

Daily Movement / Workout

1 _____ 10

Sleep

1 _____ 10

Meditation

1 _____ 10

Daily Focus:

Think of all the ways you could add more walking into your daily routine.

Scribble Scrabble:

Week: 4

Date:

Start a Movement

Plan:

Meal One:

Meal Two:

Meal Three:

Snacks:

Beverages:

Start a Movement!

How did you feel about your food today?

How did you feel about your workout today?

Feel satisfied?

1 _____ 10

Did you enjoy it?

1 _____ 10

Enjoy your food?

1 _____ 10

Do you feel energized?

1 _____ 10

Eat slow / seated?

1 _____ 10

Stick to the plan?

1 _____ 10

Overall energy:

Week: 4

"If you want to achieve a high goal, you're going to have to take some chances."
—Alberto Salazar

Date:

Power Statement:

Action Plan:

Morning Prep ○

3 Deep Breaths ○

Word of the Day:

Thoughts & Visualization

1 _____ 10

Food / Water

1 _____ 10

Daily Movement / Workout

1 _____ 10

Sleep

1 _____ 10

Meditation

1 _____ 10

Daily Focus:

Today I want you to exercise while doing household chores.

Scribble Scrabble:

Week: 4

Date:

Start a Movement

Plan:

Meal One:

Meal Two:

Meal Three:

Snacks:

Beverages:

Start a Movement!

How did you feel about your food today?

How did you feel about your workout today?

Feel satisfied?

1 _____ 10

Did you enjoy it?

1 _____ 10

Enjoy your food?

1 _____ 10

Do you feel energized?

1 _____ 10

Eat slow / seated?

1 _____ 10

Stick to the plan?

1 _____ 10

Overall energy:

"Spend most of your time thinking about what you do want. If you dwell on what you don't want, you will get more of it." —Sandy Joy Weston

Date:

Power Statement:

Action Plan:

Morning Prep ◯

3 Deep Breaths ◯

Word of the Day:

Thoughts & Visualization

1 _____ 10

Food / Water

1 _____ 10

Daily Movement / Workout

1 _____ 10

Sleep

1 _____ 10

Meditation

1 _____ 10

Daily Focus:

Today I want you to add push-ups into your routine, any kind will do.

Scribble Scrabble:

Week: 4

Date:

Start a Movement

> **Plan:**

Meal One:

Meal Two:

Meal Three:

Snacks:

Beverages:

Start a Movement!

How did you feel about your food today?

How did you feel about your workout today?

Feel satisfied?

1 _____ 10

Did you enjoy it?

1 _____ 10

Enjoy your food?

1 _____ 10

Do you feel energized?

1 _____ 10

Eat slow / seated?

1 _____ 10

Stick to the plan?

1 _____ 10

Overall energy:

Week: 4

"When you come to a roadblock, take a detour." —Mary Kay Ash

Date:

Power Statement:

Action Plan:

Morning Prep ○

3 Deep Breaths ○

Word of the Day:

Thoughts & Visualization

1 _____ 10

Food / Water

1 _____ 10

Daily Movement / Workout

1 _____ 10

Sleep

1 _____ 10

Meditation

1 _____ 10

Daily Focus:

Today I want you to do something, anything, outside.

Scribble Scrabble:

Date:

Start a Movement

Plan:

Meal One:

Meal Two:

Meal Three:

Snacks:

Beverages:

Start a Movement!

How did you feel about your food today?

How did you feel about your workout today?

Feel satisfied?

1 _____ 10

Enjoy your food?

1 _____ 10

Eat slow / seated?

1 _____ 10

Stick to the plan?

1 _____ 10

Did you enjoy it?

1 _____ 10

Do you feel energized?

1 _____ 10

Overall energy:

Week: 4

"Whenever you think people are judging you, first ask yourself, 'Am I judging myself?'" —Sandy Joy Weston

Date:

Power Statement:

Action Plan:

Morning Prep ○

3 Deep Breaths ○

Word of the Day:

Thoughts & Visualization

1 _____ 10

Food / Water

1 _____ 10

Daily Movement / Workout

1 _____ 10

Sleep

1 _____ 10

Meditation

1 _____ 10

Daily Focus:

Today I want you to try a new abdominal exercise.

Scribble Scrabble:

Date:

Start a Movement

Plan:

Meal One:

Meal Two:

Meal Three:

Snacks:

Beverages:

Start a Movement!

How did you feel about your food today?

How did you feel about your workout today?

Feel satisfied?

1 _____ 10

Enjoy your food?

1 _____ 10

Eat slow / seated?

1 _____ 10

Stick to the plan?

1 _____ 10

Did you enjoy it?

1 _____ 10

Do you feel energized?

1 _____ 10

Overall energy:

"Believe you can and you're halfway there." —Theodore Roosevelt

Date:

Power Statement:

Action Plan:

Morning Prep ○

3 Deep Breaths ○

Word of the Day:

Thoughts & Visualization

1 _____ 10

Food / Water

1 _____ 10

Daily Movement / Workout

1 _____ 10

Sleep

1 _____ 10

Meditation

1 _____ 10

Daily Focus:

Today I want you to do a new leg exercise—I love squats.

Scribble Scrabble:

Date:

Start a Movement

> **Plan:**

Meal One:

Meal Two:

Meal Three:

Snacks:

Beverages:

Start a Movement!

How did you feel about your food today?

How did you feel about your workout today?

Feel satisfied?

1 _____ 10

Did you enjoy it?

1 _____ 10

Enjoy your food?

1 _____ 10

Do you feel energized?

1 _____ 10

Eat slow / seated?

1 _____ 10

Stick to the plan?

1 _____ 10

Overall energy:

"Before you let your mind wander with all the things that could go wrong, change it up and let it wander with all the things that could go right." —Sandy Joy Weston

Big Picture Reset

What positive habits did you form in the last 30 days?

How could you adjust your schedule to fit your G.A.M.E. Plan?

How could you shift your mindset to reach your new G.A.M.E. Plan?

Week: 4

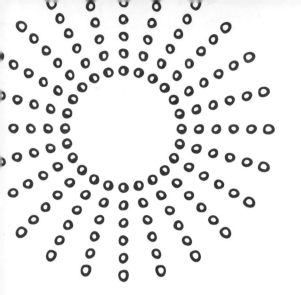

Your Second 30 Days Start Now!

What's Your G.A.M.E. Plan?

Goal

What do you want?

_____

_____

Action

What will you do the get there?

_____

_____

Motivation

Why are you really doing this?

_____

_____

Energy

How are you feeling today?

_____

_____

All it takes is 1 to 3 minutes a day to change your body and your life in a positive way!

Brain Drain

Squash those negative buggers!

Contract

I, _____, am not responsible for my pre-existing thoughts. I am only aware of them. From this day forward, I now accept who I am, how I think and what I think, and I fully embrace the idea that I can change all of these things, one word at a time. And that's awesome.

If I accept this challenge, I will set realistic goals, whether it's to run a triathlon or get my butt off the sofa for just twenty minutes. I will train my brain like an athlete. I will focus my thoughts and move my body to achieve my full potential. I will succeed because it will be a blast.

Signature: _____ Date: _____

Pre-Game

Week: 1

Theme: Mindset

This week we are going to emphasize staying in the present moment and realizing that you are in charge of your brain, your thoughts, and your day. Wow, what a wonderful thing to know, and of course there is no judgment about whatever you are thinking.

Scribble Scrabble:

"As you start to walk out on the way, the way appears." —Rumi

Date:

Power Statement:

Action Plan:

Morning Prep ○

3 Deep Breaths ○

Word of the Day:

Thoughts & Visualization

1 _____ 10

Food / Water

1 _____ 10

Daily Movement / Workout

1 _____ 10

Sleep

1 _____ 10

Meditation

1 _____ 10

Daily Focus:

Before getting out of bed, decide how you want to show up in the world.

Scribble Scrabble:

Week: 1

Date:

Mindset

Plan:

Meal One:

Meal Two:

Meal Three:

Snacks:

Beverages:

Start a Movement!

How did you feel about your food today?

How did you feel about your workout today?

Feel satisfied?

1 _____ 10

Did you enjoy it?

1 _____ 10

Enjoy your food?

1 _____ 10

Do you feel energized?

1 _____ 10

Eat slow / seated?

1 _____ 10

Stick to the plan?

1 _____ 10

Overall energy:

"Procrastination is one of the most common and deadliest of diseases and its toll on success and happiness is heavy." —Wayne Dyer

Date:

Power Statement:

Action Plan:

Morning Prep ○

3 Deep Breaths ○

Word of the Day:

Thoughts & Visualization

1 _____ 10

Food / Water

1 _____ 10

Daily Movement / Workout

1 _____ 10

Sleep

1 _____ 10

Meditation

1 _____ 10

Daily Focus:

Be aware of the thoughts in your head that don't serve you well.

Scribble Scrabble:

Date:

Mindset

Plan:

Meal One:

Meal Two:

Meal Three:

Snacks:

Beverages:

Start a Movement!

How did you feel about your food today?

How did you feel about your workout today?

Feel satisfied?

1 _____ 10

Did you enjoy it?

1 _____ 10

Enjoy your food?

1 _____ 10

Do you feel energized?

1 _____ 10

Eat slow / seated?

1 _____ 10

Stick to the plan?

1 _____ 10

Overall energy:

"Believing in yourself doesn't mean you tell people how great you are—it's just you knowing how incredible you are." —Sandy Joy Weston

Date:

Power Statement:

Action Plan:

Morning Prep ○

3 Deep Breaths ○

Word of the Day:

Thoughts & Visualization

1 _____ 10

Food / Water

1 _____ 10

Daily Movement / Workout

1 _____ 10

Sleep

1 _____ 10

Meditation

1 _____ 10

Daily Focus:

Today I want you to notice if you are staying in the present moment.

Scribble Scrabble:

Date:

Mindset

Plan:

Meal One:

Meal Two:

Meal Three:

Snacks:

Beverages:

Start a Movement!

How did you feel about your food today?

How did you feel about your workout today?

Feel satisfied?

1 _____ 10

Did you enjoy it?

1 _____ 10

Enjoy your food?

1 _____ 10

Do you feel energized?

1 _____ 10

Eat slow / seated?

1 _____ 10

Stick to the plan?

1 _____ 10

Overall energy: ⬭

Week: 1

"Sometimes life hits you in the head with a brick. Don't lose faith." —Steve Jobs

Date:

Power Statement:

Action Plan:

Morning Prep ○

3 Deep Breaths ○

Word of the Day:

Thoughts & Visualization

1 _____ 10

Food / Water

1 _____ 10

Daily Movement / Workout

1 _____ 10

Sleep

1 _____ 10

Meditation

1 _____ 10

Daily Focus:

Today I want you to say your power statement out loud throughout the day.

Scribble Scrabble:

Date:

Mindset

Plan:

Meal One:

Meal Two:

Meal Three:

Snacks:

Beverages:

Start a Movement!

How did you feel about your food today?

How did you feel about your workout today?

Feel satisfied?

1 _____ 10

Did you enjoy it?

1 _____ 10

Enjoy your food?

1 _____ 10

Do you feel energized?

1 _____ 10

Eat slow / seated?

1 _____ 10

Stick to the plan?

1 _____ 10

Overall energy:

Week: 1

"Sleep is the best meditation." —Dalai Lama

Date:

Power Statement:

Action Plan:

Morning Prep ◯

3 Deep Breaths ◯

Word of the Day:

Thoughts & Visualization

1 _____ 10

Food / Water

1 _____ 10

Daily Movement / Workout

1 _____ 10

Sleep

1 _____ 10

Meditation

1 _____ 10

Daily Focus:

Today I want you to focus on all the things you *can* do.

Scribble Scrabble:

Week: 1

Date:

Mindset

Plan:

Meal One:

Meal Two:

Meal Three:

Snacks:

Beverages:

Start a Movement!

How did you feel about your food today?

How did you feel about your workout today?

Feel satisfied?

1 _____ 10

Did you enjoy it?

1 _____ 10

Enjoy your food?

1 _____ 10

Do you feel energized?

1 _____ 10

Eat slow / seated?

1 _____ 10

Stick to the plan?

1 _____ 10

Overall energy:

Week: 1

"All that we are is the result of what we have thought." —Buddha

Date:

Power Statement:

Action Plan:

Morning Prep ○

3 Deep Breaths ○

Word of the Day:

```
Thoughts & Visualization
1 _____ 10

        Food / Water
1 _____ 10

  Daily Movement / Workout
1 _____ 10

            Sleep
1 _____ 10

         Meditation
1 _____ 10
```

Daily Focus:

Think of an area that is tough for you and then write down all the possible solutions.

Scribble Scrabble:

Date:

Mindset

Plan:

Meal One:

Meal Two:

Meal Three:

Snacks:

Beverages:

Start a Movement!

How did you feel about your food today?

How did you feel about your workout today?

Feel satisfied?

1 _____ 10

Did you enjoy it?

1 _____ 10

Enjoy your food?

1 _____ 10

Do you feel energized?

1 _____ 10

Eat slow / seated?

1 _____ 10

Stick to the plan?

1 _____ 10

Overall energy:

"If a belief is just a thought you keep repeating over and over again in your head, then doesn't it make sense to have thoughts that serve you well?" —Sandy Joy Weston

Date:

Power Statement:

Action Plan:

Morning Prep ◯

3 Deep Breaths ◯

Word of the Day:

Thoughts & Visualization

1 _____ 10

Food / Water

1 _____ 10

Daily Movement / Workout

1 _____ 10

Sleep

1 _____ 10

Meditation

1 _____ 10

Daily Focus:

Today I want you to focus on something new you've accomplished with your body.

Scribble Scrabble:

Date:

Mindset

Plan:

Meal One:

Meal Two:

Meal Three:

Snacks:

Beverages:

Start a Movement!

How did you feel about your food today?

How did you feel about your workout today?

Feel satisfied?

1 _____ 10

Enjoy your food?

1 _____ 10

Eat slow / seated?

1 _____ 10

Stick to the plan?

1 _____ 10

Did you enjoy it?

1 _____ 10

Do you feel energized?

1 _____ 10

Overall energy:

> **"Our lives begin to end the day we become silent about things that matter."**
> **—Martin Luther King, Jr.**

Reset Your Head

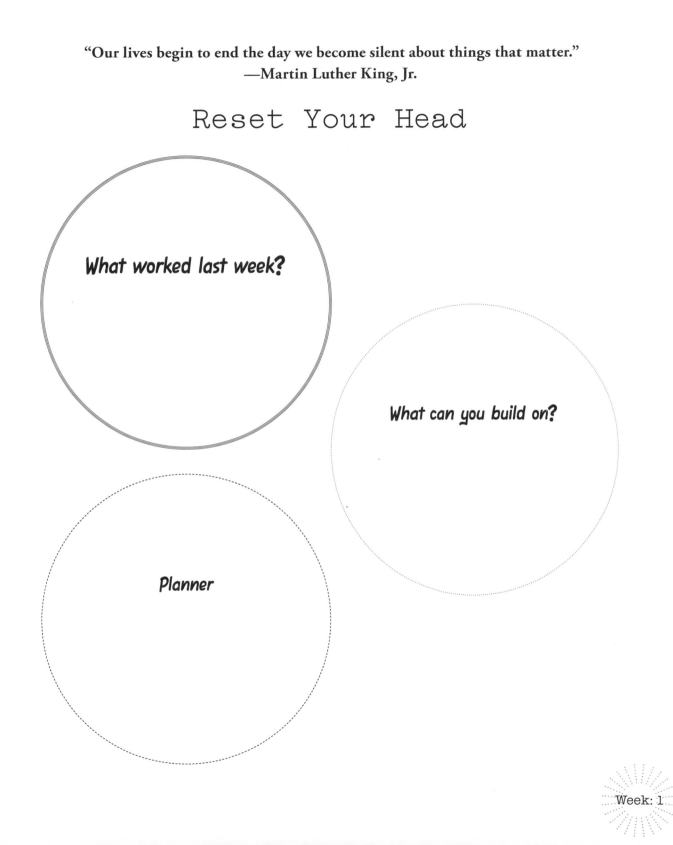

What worked last week?

What can you build on?

Planner

Pre-Game

Week: 2

Theme: Food Freedom

This week we are going to create balance and moderation with our food by not eating as much of the stuff that is not on your plan. You want to replace and replenish with food that is good for you and fun to make.

Scribble Scrabble:

"Meditate . . . do not delay, lest you later regret it." —Buddha

Date:

Power Statement:

Action Plan:

Morning Prep ○

3 Deep Breaths ○

Word of the Day:

Thoughts & Visualization

1 _____ 10

Food / Water

1 _____ 10

Daily Movement / Workout

1 _____ 10

Sleep

1 _____ 10

Meditation

1 _____ 10

Daily Focus:

Today I want you to buy food that makes you feel good inside and out.

Scribble Scrabble:

Date:

Food Freedom

Plan:

Meal One:

Meal Two:

Meal Three:

Snacks:

Beverages:

Start a Movement!

How did you feel about your food today?

How did you feel about your workout today?

Feel satisfied?

1 _____ 10

Enjoy your food?

1 _____ 10

Eat slow / seated?

1 _____ 10

Stick to the plan?

1 _____ 10

Did you enjoy it?

1 _____ 10

Do you feel energized?

1 _____ 10

Overall energy:

Week: 2

"The most difficult thing is the decision to act, the rest is merely tenacity."
—Amelia Earhart

Date:

Power Statement:

Action Plan:

Morning Prep ○

3 Deep Breaths ○

Word of the Day:

Thoughts & Visualization

1 _____ 10

Food / Water

1 _____ 10

Daily Movement / Workout

1 _____ 10

Sleep

1 _____ 10

Meditation

1 _____ 10

Daily Focus:

Today I want you to prepare food
that you could eat throughout week.

Scribble Scrabble:

Date:

Food Freedom

Plan:

Meal One:

Meal Two:

Meal Three:

Snacks:

Beverages:

Start a Movement!

How did you feel about your food today?

How did you feel about your workout today?

Feel satisfied?

1 _____ 10

Enjoy your food?

1 _____ 10

Eat slow / seated?

1 _____ 10

Stick to the plan?

1 _____ 10

Did you enjoy it?

1 _____ 10

Do you feel energized?

1 _____ 10

Overall energy:

Week: 2

"I am not perfect, but I am amazing; you are not perfect, but you are amazing."
—Sandy Joy Weston

Date:

Power Statement:

Action Plan:

Morning Prep ○

3 Deep Breaths ○

Word of the Day:

Thoughts & Visualization
1 _____ 10

Food / Water
1 _____ 10

Daily Movement / Workout
1 _____ 10

Sleep
1 _____ 10

Meditation
1 _____ 10

Daily Focus:

Today I want you to treat yourself to takeout that fits your plan.

Scribble Scrabble:

Week: 2

Date:

Food Freedom

Plan:

Meal One:

Meal Two:

Meal Three:

Snacks:

Beverages:

Start a Movement!

How did you feel about your food today?

How did you feel about your workout today?

Feel satisfied?

1 _____ 10

Did you enjoy it?

1 _____ 10

Enjoy your food?

1 _____ 10

Do you feel energized?

1 _____ 10

Eat slow / seated?

1 _____ 10

Stick to the plan?

1 _____ 10

Overall energy:

"Action is the foundational key to all success." —Pablo Picasso

Date:

Power Statement:

Action Plan:

Morning Prep ○

3 Deep Breaths ○

Word of the Day:

Thoughts & Visualization

1 _____ 10

Food / Water

1 _____ 10

Daily Movement / Workout

1 _____ 10

Sleep

1 _____ 10

Meditation

1 _____ 10

Daily Focus:

Explore another healthy way of eating.

Scribble Scrabble:

Date:

Food Freedom

Plan:

Meal One:

Meal Two:

Meal Three:

Snacks:

Beverages:

Start a Movement!

How did you feel about your food today?

How did you feel about your workout today?

Feel satisfied?

1 _____ 10

Did you enjoy it?

1 _____ 10

Enjoy your food?

1 _____ 10

Do you feel energized?

1 _____ 10

Eat slow / seated?

1 _____ 10

Stick to the plan?

1 _____ 10

Overall energy:

"Someday is not a day of the week." —Denise Brennan-Nelson

Date:

Power Statement:

Action Plan:

Morning Prep ◯

3 Deep Breaths ◯

Word of the Day:

Thoughts & Visualization

1 _____ 10

Food / Water

1 _____ 10

Daily Movement / Workout

1 _____ 10

Sleep

1 _____ 10

Meditation

1 _____ 10

Daily Focus:

Try one new healthy recipe today.

Scribble Scrabble:

Week: 2

Date:

Food Freedom

Plan:

Meal One:

Meal Two:

Meal Three:

Snacks:

Beverages:

Start a Movement!

How did you feel about your food today?

How did you feel about your workout today?

Feel satisfied?

1 _____ 10

Enjoy your food?

1 _____ 10

Eat slow / seated?

1 _____ 10

Stick to the plan?

1 _____ 10

Did you enjoy it?

1 _____ 10

Do you feel energized?

1 _____ 10

Overall energy:

"Life is 10 percent what happens to you and 90 percent how you react to it." —Charles Swindoll

Date:

Power Statement:

Action Plan:

Morning Prep ◯

3 Deep Breaths ◯

Word of the Day:

Thoughts & Visualization

1 _____ 10

Food / Water

1 _____ 10

Daily Movement / Workout

1 _____ 10

Sleep

1 _____ 10

Meditation

1 _____ 10

Daily Focus:

Cut one thing out of your food plan that doesn't serve you well.

Scribble Scrabble:

Date:

Food Freedom

Plan:

Meal One:

Meal Two:

Meal Three:

Snacks:

Beverages:

Start a Movement!

How did you feel about your food today?

How did you feel about your workout today?

Feel satisfied?

1 _____ 10

Did you enjoy it?

1 _____ 10

Enjoy your food?

1 _____ 10

Do you feel energized?

1 _____ 10

Eat slow / seated?

1 _____ 10

Stick to the plan?

1 _____ 10

Overall energy:

Week: 2

"Don't judge each day by the harvest you reap but by the seeds that you plant."
—Robert Louis Stevenson

Date:

Power Statement:

Action Plan:

Morning Prep ○	
3 Deep Breaths ○	
Word of the Day:	

Thoughts & Visualization

1 _____ 10

Food / Water

1 _____ 10

Daily Movement / Workout

1 _____ 10

Sleep

1 _____ 10

Meditation

1 _____ 10

Daily Focus:

Show extra gratitude for the food you are going to eat.

Scribble Scrabble:

Date:

Food Freedom

Plan:

Meal One:

Meal Two:

Meal Three:

Snacks:

Beverages:

Start a Movement!

How did you feel about your food today?

How did you feel about your workout today?

Feel satisfied?

1 _____ 10

Did you enjoy it?

1 _____ 10

Enjoy your food?

1 _____ 10

Do you feel energized?

1 _____ 10

Eat slow / seated?

1 _____ 10

Stick to the plan?

1 _____ 10

Overall energy:

"The world doesn't happen to you, you happen to the world. You choose how you show up in the world. If you choose love, then the world will reflect love." —Sandy Joy Weston

Reset Your Head

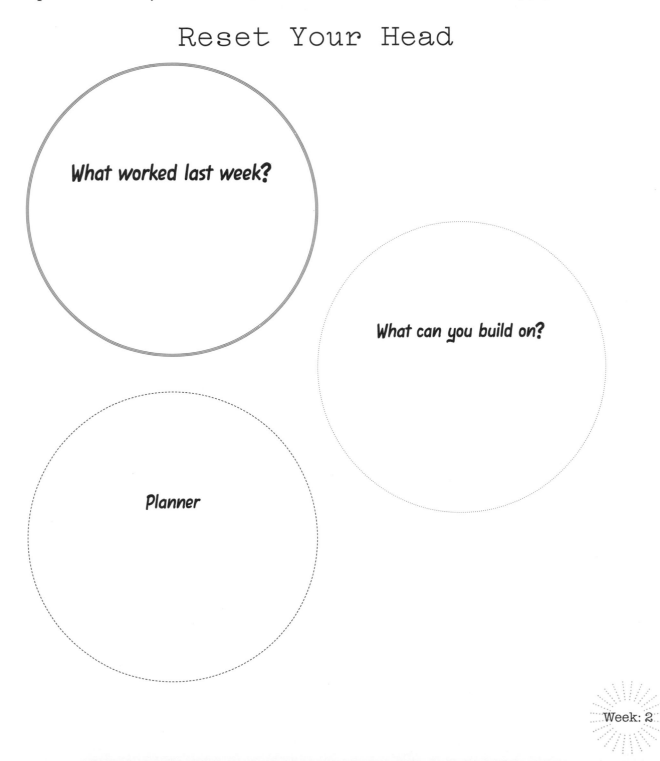

What worked last week?

What can you build on?

Planner

Pre-Game

Week: 3

Theme: Spiritual Life Balance

This week we are going to go just a bit deeper with your spiritual life balance and find different ways to keep you grounded.

> *Scribble Scrabble:*

"When everything seems to be going against you, remember that the airplane takes off against the wind, not with it." —Henry Ford

Date:

Power Statement:

Action Plan:

Morning Prep ○

3 Deep Breaths ○

Word of the Day:

Thoughts & Visualization

1 _____ 10

Food / Water

1 _____ 10

Daily Movement / Workout

1 _____ 10

Sleep

1 _____ 10

Meditation

1 _____ 10

Daily Focus:

Today I want you to meditate for
1 minute throughout your day when
needed.

Scribble Scrabble:

Date:

Spiritual Life Balance

Plan:

Meal One:

Meal Two:

Meal Three:

Snacks:

Beverages:

Start a Movement!

How did you feel about your food today?

How did you feel about your workout today?

Feel satisfied?

1 _____ 10

Did you enjoy it?

1 _____ 10

Enjoy your food?

1 _____ 10

Do you feel energized?

1 _____ 10

Eat slow / seated?

1 _____ 10

Stick to the plan?

1 _____ 10

Overall energy:

Week: 3

"The point of power is always in the present moment." —Louise Hay

Date:

Power Statement:

Action Plan:

Morning Prep ◯	
3 Deep Breaths ◯	
Word of the Day:	

Thoughts & Visualization

1 _____ 10

Food / Water

1 _____ 10

Daily Movement / Workout

1 _____ 10

Sleep

1 _____ 10

Meditation

1 _____ 10

Daily Focus:

Today I want you to give yourself a big giant hug.

Scribble Scrabble:

Date:

Spiritual Life Balance

Plan:

Meal One:

Meal Two:

Meal Three:

Snacks:

Beverages:

Start a Movement!

How did you feel about your food today?

How did you feel about your workout today?

Feel satisfied?

1 _____ 10

Did you enjoy it?

1 _____ 10

Enjoy your food?

1 _____ 10

Do you feel energized?

1 _____ 10

Eat slow / seated?

1 _____ 10

Stick to the plan?

1 _____ 10

Overall energy:

"I can accept failure, everyone fails at something. But I can't accept not trying."
—Michael Jordan

Date:

Power Statement:

Action Plan:

Morning Prep ◯

3 Deep Breaths ◯

Word of the Day:

Thoughts & Visualization

1 _____ 10

Food / Water

1 _____ 10

Daily Movement / Workout

1 _____ 10

Sleep

1 _____ 10

Meditation

1 _____ 10

Daily Focus:

Accept yourself for who you are right now.

Scribble Scrabble:

Date:

Spiritual Life Balance

Plan:

Meal One:

Meal Two:

Meal Three:

Snacks:

Beverages:

Start a Movement!

How did you feel about your food today?

How did you feel about your workout today?

Feel satisfied?

1 _____ 10

Did you enjoy it?

1 _____ 10

Enjoy your food?

1 _____ 10

Do you feel energized?

1 _____ 10

Eat slow / seated?

1 _____ 10

Stick to the plan?

1 _____ 10

Overall energy:

Week: 3

"What you seek is seeking you." —Rumi

Date:

Power Statement:

Action Plan:

Morning Prep ○

3 Deep Breaths ○

Word of the Day:

Thoughts & Visualization

1 _____ 10

Food / Water

1 _____ 10

Daily Movement / Workout

1 _____ 10

Sleep

1 _____ 10

Meditation

1 _____ 10

Daily Focus:

Today, I want to find a few minutes to play some mellow music and relax.

Scribble Scrabble:

Date:

Spiritual Life Balance

Plan:

Meal One:

Meal Two:

Meal Three:

Snacks:

Beverages:

Start a Movement!

How did you feel about your food today?

How did you feel about your workout today?

Feel satisfied?

1 _____ 10

Did you enjoy it?

1 _____ 10

Enjoy your food?

1 _____ 10

Do you feel energized?

1 _____ 10

Eat slow / seated?

1 _____ 10

Stick to the plan?

1 _____ 10

Overall energy:

"In order to grow you must take risks and believe in yourself, always."
—Sandy Joy Weston

Date:

Power Statement:

Action Plan:

Morning Prep ◯

3 Deep Breaths ◯

Word of the Day:

Thoughts & Visualization

1 _____ 10

Food / Water

1 _____ 10

Daily Movement / Workout

1 _____ 10

Sleep

1 _____ 10

Meditation

1 _____ 10

Daily Focus:

Plan out your day so that you can experience it with ease and flow.

Scribble Scrabble:

Date:

Spiritual Life Balance

Plan:

Meal One:

Meal Two:

Meal Three:

Snacks:

Beverages:

Start a Movement!

How did you feel about your food today?

How did you feel about your workout today?

Feel satisfied?

1 _____ 10

Enjoy your food?

1 _____ 10

Eat slow / seated?

1 _____ 10

Stick to the plan?

1 _____ 10

Did you enjoy it?

1 _____ 10

Do you feel energized?

1 _____ 10

Overall energy:

"Love is the absence of judgment." —Dalai Lama

Date:

Power Statement:

Action Plan:

Morning Prep ○

3 Deep Breaths ○

Word of the Day:

Thoughts & Visualization

1 _____ 10

Food / Water

1 _____ 10

Daily Movement / Workout

1 _____ 10

Sleep

1 _____ 10

Meditation

1 _____ 10

Daily Focus:

Find 5 minutes and just breathe and reconnect to your goals.

Scribble Scrabble:

Week: 3

Date:

Spiritual Life Balance

Plan:

Meal One:

Meal Two:

Meal Three:

Snacks:

Beverages:

Start a Movement!

How did you feel about your food today?

How did you feel about your workout today?

Feel satisfied?

1 _____ 10

Did you enjoy it?

1 _____ 10

Enjoy your food?

1 _____ 10

Do you feel energized?

1 _____ 10

Eat slow / seated?

1 _____ 10

Stick to the plan?

1 _____ 10

Overall energy:

"My day begins and ends with gratitude and joy." —Louise Hay

Date:

Power Statement:

Action Plan:

Morning Prep ○

3 Deep Breaths ○

Word of the Day:

Thoughts & Visualization

1 _____ 10

Food / Water

1 _____ 10

Daily Movement / Workout

1 _____ 10

Sleep

1 _____ 10

Meditation

1 _____ 10

Daily Focus:

Today remind yourself that there is nothing more important than you feeling good.

Scribble Scrabble:

Date:

Spiritual Life Balance

Plan:

Meal One:

Meal Two:

Meal Three:

Snacks:

Beverages:

Start a Movement!

How did you feel about your food today?

How did you feel about your workout today?

Feel satisfied?

1 _____ 10

Did you enjoy it?

1 _____ 10

Enjoy your food?

1 _____ 10

Do you feel energized?

1 _____ 10

Eat slow / seated?

1 _____ 10

Stick to the plan?

1 _____ 10

Overall energy: ◯

"If you want different, you have to think and act different." —Pat Croce

Reset Your Head

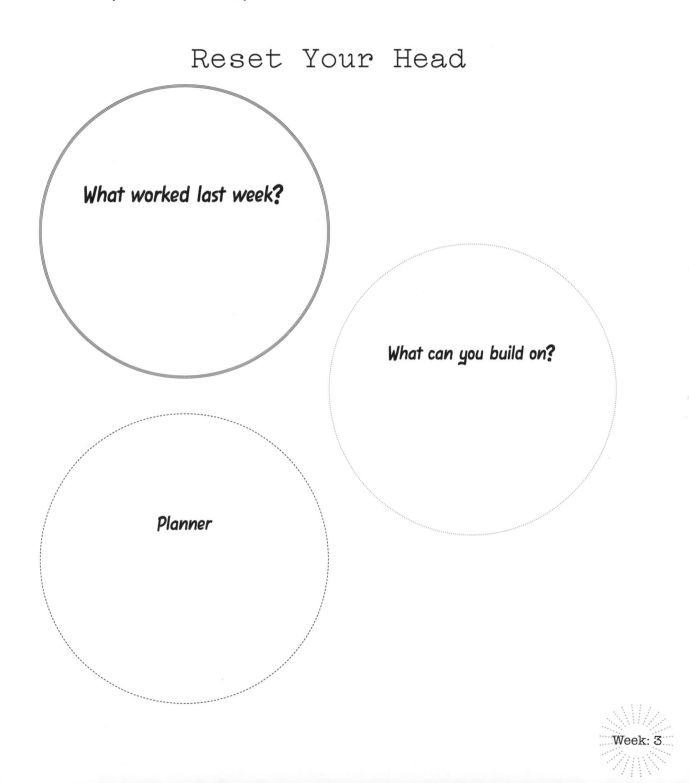

What worked last week?

What can you build on?

Planner

Pre-Game

Week: 4

Theme: Start a Movement

Okay superstar, let's keep this party moving and take it up a notch. Now that you know what you like and don't like it should be easy peasy to add on to your program. I am sure you've found plenty of things that make you want to move.

Scribble Scrabble:

"Close your eyes and visualize the life you want to live today." —Sandy Joy Weston

Date:

Power Statement:

Action Plan:

Morning Prep ○

3 Deep Breaths ○

Word of the Day:

Thoughts & Visualization

1 _____ 10

Food / Water

1 _____ 10

Daily Movement / Workout

1 _____ 10

Sleep

1 _____ 10

Meditation

1 _____ 10

Daily Focus:

Try a brand-new workout at home or the gym.

Scribble Scrabble:

Date:

Start a Movement

Plan:

Meal One:

Meal Two:

Meal Three:

Snacks:

Beverages:

Start a Movement!

How did you feel about your food today?

How did you feel about your workout today?

Feel satisfied?

1 _____ 10

Did you enjoy it?

1 _____ 10

Enjoy your food?

1 _____ 10

Do you feel energized?

1 _____ 10

Eat slow / seated?

1 _____ 10

Stick to the plan?

1 _____ 10

Overall energy:

"I will go anywhere as long as it is forward." —David Livingstone

Date:

Power Statement:

Action Plan:

Morning Prep ○

3 Deep Breaths ○

Word of the Day:

Thoughts & Visualization

1 _____ 10

Food / Water

1 _____ 10

Daily Movement / Workout

1 _____ 10

Sleep

1 _____ 10

Meditation

1 _____ 10

Daily Focus:

Today, I want you to do a workout routine that emphasizes your upper body.

Scribble Scrabble:

Week: 4

Date:

Start a Movement

Plan:

Meal One:

Meal Two:

Meal Three:

Snacks:

Beverages:

Start a Movement!

How did you feel about your food today?

How did you feel about your workout today?

Feel satisfied?

1 _____ 10

Did you enjoy it?

1 _____ 10

Enjoy your food?

1 _____ 10

Do you feel energized?

1 _____ 10

Eat slow / seated?

1 _____ 10

Stick to the plan?

1 _____ 10

Overall energy:

Week: 4

"Practice puts brains in your muscles." —Sam Snead

Date:

Power Statement:

Action Plan:

Morning Prep ○

3 Deep Breaths ○

Word of the Day:

Thoughts & Visualization

1 _____ 10

Food / Water

1 _____ 10

Daily Movement / Workout

1 _____ 10

Sleep

1 _____ 10

Meditation

1 _____ 10

Daily Focus:

Try a few minutes of planks (if you aren't sure, just google them).

Scribble Scrabble:

Week: 4

Date:

Start a Movement

Plan:

Meal One:

Meal Two:

Meal Three:

Snacks:

Beverages:

Start a Movement!

How did you feel about your food today?

How did you feel about your workout today?

Feel satisfied?

1 _____ 10

Did you enjoy it?

1 _____ 10

Enjoy your food?

1 _____ 10

Do you feel energized?

1 _____ 10

Eat slow / seated?

1 _____ 10

Stick to the plan?

1 _____ 10

Overall energy: ◯

"The best abs exercise is 5 sets of stop eating so much crap." —Lazar Angelov

Date:

Power Statement:

Action Plan:

Morning Prep ○

3 Deep Breaths ○

Word of the Day:

Thoughts & Visualization

1 _____ 10

Food / Water

1 _____ 10

Daily Movement / Workout

1 _____ 10

Sleep

1 _____ 10

Meditation

1 _____ 10

Daily Focus:

Today, I want you to do a workout routine that emphasizes your lower body.

Scribble Scrabble:

Week: 4

Date:

Start a Movement

Plan:

Meal One:

Meal Two:

Meal Three:

Snacks:

Beverages:

Start a Movement!

How did you feel about your food today?

How did you feel about your workout today?

Feel satisfied?

1 _____ 10

Did you enjoy it?

1 _____ 10

Enjoy your food?

1 _____ 10

Do you feel energized?

1 _____ 10

Eat slow / seated?

1 _____ 10

Stick to the plan?

1 _____ 10

Overall energy:

"Breathe, meditate, and always communicate." —Sandy Joy Weston

Date:

Power Statement:

Action Plan:

Morning Prep ○

3 Deep Breaths ○

Word of the Day:

Thoughts & Visualization

1 _____ 10

Food / Water

1 _____ 10

Daily Movement / Workout

1 _____ 10

Sleep

1 _____ 10

Meditation

1 _____ 10

Daily Focus:

Today, I want you to do a few more minutes of yoga or stretching.

Scribble Scrabble:

Week: 4

Date:

Start a Movement

Plan:

Meal One:

Meal Two:

Meal Three:

Snacks:

Beverages:

Start a Movement!

How did you feel about your food today?

How did you feel about your workout today?

Feel satisfied?

1 _____ 10

Did you enjoy it?

1 _____ 10

Enjoy your food?

1 _____ 10

Do you feel energized?

1 _____ 10

Eat slow / seated?

1 _____ 10

Stick to the plan?

1 _____ 10

Overall energy:

"Change will not come if we wait for some other person or some other time."
—Barack Obama

Date:

Power Statement:

Action Plan:

Morning Prep ○

3 Deep Breaths ○

Word of the Day:

Thoughts & Visualization

1 _____ 10

Food / Water

1 _____ 10

Daily Movement / Workout

1 _____ 10

Sleep

1 _____ 10

Meditation

1 _____ 10

Daily Focus:

Work out with a friend today.

Scribble Scrabble:

Week: 4

Date:

Start a Movement

> **Plan:**

Meal One:

Meal Two:

Meal Three:

Snacks:

Beverages:

Start a Movement!

How did you feel about your food today?

How did you feel about your workout today?

Feel satisfied?

1 _____ 10

Did you enjoy it?

1 _____ 10

Enjoy your food?

1 _____ 10

Do you feel energized?

1 _____ 10

Eat slow / seated?

1 _____ 10

Stick to the plan?

1 _____ 10

Overall energy: ◯

"Very often a change of self is needed more than a change of scene."
—Arthur Christopher Benson

Date:

Power Statement:

Action Plan:

	Morning Prep ○
	3 Deep Breaths ○
	Word of the Day:

Thoughts & Visualization
1 _____ 10

Food / Water
1 _____ 10

Daily Movement / Workout
1 _____ 10

Sleep
1 _____ 10

Meditation
1 _____ 10

Daily Focus:

Today, I want you to act like a kid and do movement that is fun. Dance, jungle gym, run around, etc.

Scribble Scrabble:

Date:

Start a Movement

Plan:

Meal One:

Meal Two:

Meal Three:

Snacks:

Beverages:

Start a Movement!

How did you feel about your food today?

How did you feel about your workout today?

Feel satisfied?

1 _____ 10

Did you enjoy it?

1 _____ 10

Enjoy your food?

1 _____ 10

Do you feel energized?

1 _____ 10

Eat slow / seated?

1 _____ 10

Stick to the plan?

1 _____ 10

Overall energy:

> *"When you want something, all the universe conspires in helping you to achieve it."*
> —Paulo Coelho

Reset Your Head

What positive habits did you form in the last 30 days?

How could you adjust your schedule to fit your G.A.M.E. Plan?

How could you shift your mindset to reach your new G.A.M.E. Plan?

Week: 4

Big Picture Reset

What positive habits did you form in the last 30 days?

How could you adjust your schedule to fit your G.A.M.E. Plan?

How could you shift your mindset to reach your new G.A.M.E. Plan?

Week: 4

It's Your Turn!

Well my new friends, I think you are ready. Ready to conquer this new chapter of your lives with joy and excitement for what's to come. Your last 30-day journal is up to you.

I want you to take everything you've learned and enjoyed from the last 60 days and mash it up into an awesome, personalized 30-day journal of your own creation. Make sure you choose cover art that inspires you and a journal size to fit your needs. This can even extend past your 30-days and be your new daily journal. Remember, the sky's the limit, be as creative as possible!

I highly recommend my journal as a base but you can change it up if you want—do what feels right for you. You can check out www.sandyjoy-weston.com for some other fun journal ideas as well.

Let the fun begin!

Knowledge Junky: Recommended Reading

Mindset:
Wired for Joy by Laurel Mellin
Big Magic by Elizabeth Gilbert
Learned Optimism by Martin E. P. Seligman
The Inner Matrix by Joey Klein

Food Freedom:
The Ultimate Grain-Free Cookbook by Annabelle Lee
Eat Pretty by Jolene Hart
Food: What The Heck Should I Eat? by Mark Hyman
I Quit Sugar by Sarah Wilson

Spiritual Life Balance:
The Universe Has Your Back by Gabrielle Bernstein
You Can Heal Your Life by Louise Hay
Ask and It Is Given by Esther and Jerry Hicks
Excuses Begone! by Wayne Dyer

Start a Movement:
Train Your Head & Your Body Will Follow by Sandy Joy Weston
ROAR by Stacy Sims
The Men's Fitness Exercise Bible by Sean Hyson
Just Move! by James P. Owen

Weston's Words

To my amazing journalers,

You are ready, go do your thing!

    I hope you found these journals helpful in all areas of well-being. I also hope you laughed a lot and didn't take any of this too seriously. My words of wisdom are guides for you to make changes to your life that serve you well and feel good to you.

    You are an incredible human being who will continue on in your journey, your way. You can't get it wrong; it's impossible. Sure, you might take some twists and turns and maybe even go off a cliff or two, but so what? It is your life and you are in charge of your thoughts and your body. You have the power and the strength to carve out your slice of this world. You are not here to be perfect, you are here to live, live, live. That is what makes you freaking awesome. You can't go back now, you know too much. You know what it feels like to feel good and that is all that matters.

    I want to thank you for taking this journey with me and letting me share a bit of myself with you. Just knowing that I could touch someone's life, for even a moment, in a positive way just gives me goosebumps. We are all in this together. I do believe energy can be felt and travels fast and furiously. I send you unconditional loving thoughts and I hope I have inspired you to live large and feel joy as much as possible.

Many blessings,
Sandy Joy Weston

P.S. I really hope you continue on with journaling . . . *All it takes is 1 to 3 minutes a day to change your body, your life, in a positive way.*

Notes

....

....

....

....

....

....

....

....

....

....

....

Notes

....

....

....

....

....

....

....

....

....

....

....

....

Notes

....

....

....

....

....

....

....

....

....

....

....

....